puke: /pyo͞ok/ verb

vomit; spew; disgorge the contents of one's stomach

Etymology:

Probably of imitative origin; German: spucken "to spit"
Latin: spuere

First recorded use circa 1600

"At first the infant, mewling and puking in the nurse's arms"
                                            -William Shakespeare

Everyone
Pukes

Written and Illustrated
by Aunt Natalie

Little Storm Publishing
New York, NY

Adam,
If Birthdays
Bring Cheer,
What do the other
days Bring?
Hopefully Good Beer!!
all the Best,
Aunt Natalie

Everyone Pukes

Copyright © 2013 Natalie Burgess

Little Storm Publishing
New York, NY
www.littlestormpublishing.com

First Edition

ISBN: 978-0-9899456-0-8
Library of Congress Control Number: 2013920538

www.facebook.com/EveryonePukes

Did you know that everyone pukes?

It's true,

from popes to politicians,

pop stars, princesses,

physicists,

even you.

Your Momma puked
when you were growing inside of her belly.

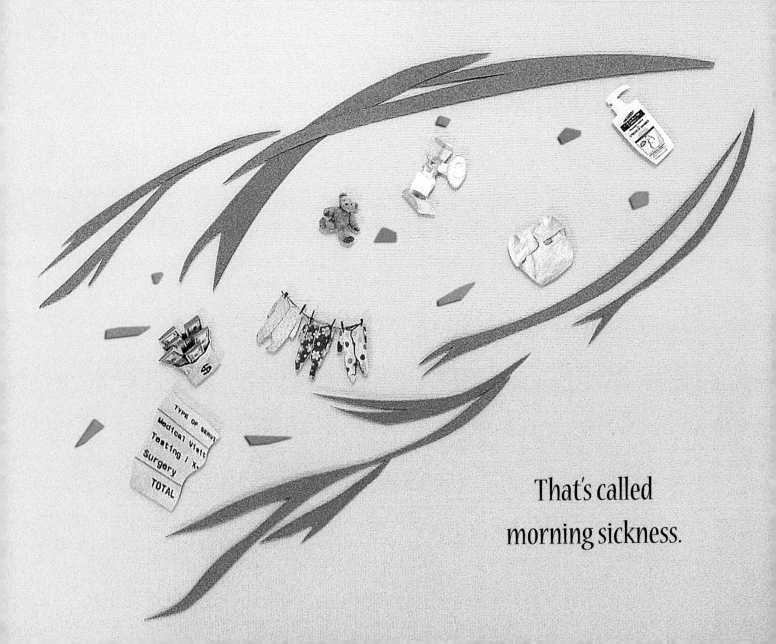

That's called
morning sickness.

Kids puke
  all the time,

and for all
   sorts of reasons.

Suspiciously skinny Sally pukes after every meal.

That's called bulimia.

I wish she wouldn't do that! It's not good for her and she looks lovely with curves.

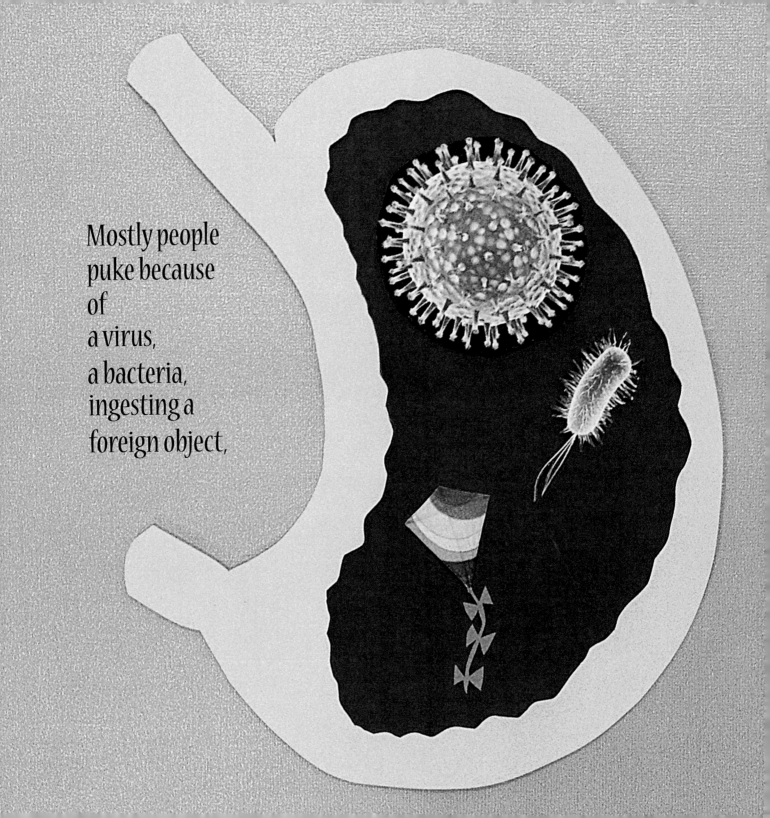

Mostly people
puke because
of
a virus,
a bacteria,
ingesting a
foreign object,

That's   Called   Alcohol

Raw Materials
Fruits and grains
high in sugar are made
into a juicy mash

+

Fermentation
Yeast is added and converts
the sugars into energy

=

Alcohol
Ethyl alcohol and
carbon dioxide
are the waste products

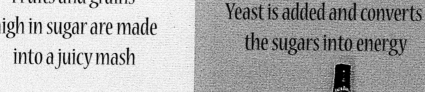  

Distillation
=
Spirits and Liquors
=
CH_3CH_2OH

The fermented product
is boiled and the vapor
cooled and collected

The result is a highly concentrated
alcoholic beverage.
AKA Booze, Hooch, Sauce

Alcohol
is
yeast poop!

... and it can really make you puke.

Big Jake puked
at last week's kegger,

Katy had to keep creepy Charlie from creeping on Charlene.

After getting rid of Charlie, Katy made sure Charlene was coherent. Then Katy turned Charlene on to her side to sleep so she wouldn't choke on her own puke and die.

That's called taking care of business.

Jimi Hendrix,
John Bonham,
and the singer
from AC/DC
all puked.

The coroner calls that
pulmonary aspiration of vomit.
A tragedy by any other name.

Sometimes people don't puke,

but it still doesn't end well.

We lay to rest
young Harold Chung.
He drank 21 shots of rum.
His 21st Birthday
wasn't much fun.
No one did call 911.

There are
no words for this.

The Six Stages of Inebriation

If a little makes you feel good, a lot will make you feel better...right?

Effects

Drinks Per Hour *

Relaxed
and feeling good

Heightened emotions,
making bad choices, beer goggles

Lack of coordination,
prone to injury, stop drinking

Puking is certain,
don't leave your friend alone

Unresponsive,
Get medical help immediately

- Euphoria
- Excitement
- Confusion
- Stupor
- Coma
- Death

Don't let a good time turn into a tragic time.

*Everyone has a different tolerance, but no matter
how big and burly you are, the human body can only metabolize
about one drink per hour, beyond that you are in**toxic**ated.

Go ahead, celebrate, revel, have fun.

Don't drink till you puke, know when you're done.

There's no shame in saying "I've reached my limit."

Come the next morning you'll be happy you did it.

You're playing with poison, please, check your friends twice.

So have a good time and follow this good advice:

DO enjoy a campfire with friends by a lake or the ocean.

DON'T go swimming.

DO enjoy the view and take pictures from a safe distance.

DON'T sit on railings and ledges or lean out of windows.

DO enjoy a cozy night in the back of your car or the cab of your wheat harvester.

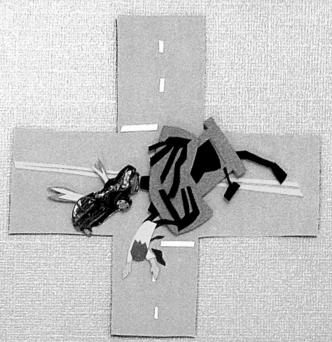

DON'T operate heavy machinery such as a car or wheat harvester.

DO enjoy watching your friends dance around like they just don't care.

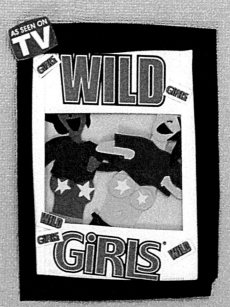

DON'T let them do this.

Author's Note

Thank you to the anonymous young man
who saved the life of someone very close to me.

Many years ago, she drank much too much
much too fast at a party.
Unfortunately, no one stopped the creepy Charlie.

Luckily, a young man did turn her on to her side
when she started to puke.
He knew to do this because a friend of his
had died in the same manner.

These are hard ways for young folks to learn simple lessons.

Made in the USA
Middletown, DE
21 January 2015